What are we doing to our kids?

Compiled and edited by

John Osmond,
Director, IWA

Nick Morris,
Research Officer, IWA

CW00606365

Commissioned by

March 2009

Sefydliad Materion Cymreig
Institute of Welsh Affairs

The Institute of Welsh Affairs exists to promote quality research and informed debate affecting the cultural, social, political and economic well-being of Wales. IWA is an independent organisation owing no allegiance to any political or economic interest group. Our only interest is in seeing Wales flourish as a country in which to work and live. We are funded by a range of organisations and individuals. For more information about the Institute, its publications, and how to join, either as an individual or corporate supporter, contact:

IWA - Institute of Welsh Affairs
4 Cathedral Road
Cardiff
CF11 9LJ

tel   029 2066 0820
fax   029 2023 3741
email wales@iwa.org.uk
web   www.iwa.org.uk

Contents

1   Preface

4   Introduction

8   Chapter 1   Family Life and Relationships

19   Chapter 2   Play and Freedom

34   Chapter 3   Boundaries And Rules

44   Chapter 4   The Future

51   Chapter 5   Findings

62   Chapter 6   Commentary

62   Let's get talking
Keith Towler, Children's Commissioner for Wales

64   Diverse Childhoods, Participation and Democracy:
Some reasons to be cheerful
Sally Holland, School of Social Sciences, Cardiff University

66   Freedom to play
Mike Greenaway, Director, Play Wales

69   A need to address gender differences and children's fears
Catriona Williams, Chief Executive, Children in Wales

72   Appendix 1
Outline Profiles of the Schools Involved in the Study

73   Appendix 2
Project Steering Group

Preface

What are doing to our kids? is a question BBC Cymru Wales is posing in a season of output in late March 2009 which will look at childhood in Wales today. The season has been prompted by a number of reports which have sounded alarms about the well-being of children and young people in the UK. In 2007 the UK came bottom of a Unicef league table which measured and compared the state of childhood in 21 industrialised countries. This negative assessment of the quality of modern British childhood has been reinforced by the findings of the Good Childhood Inquiry, conducted by the Children's Society and published in February 2009.

With these troubling assessments as a backdrop, we decided to turn a spotlight on childhood in a season across BBC Cymru Wales TV, radio and online services. The aim is to push the issues higher up the public agenda and facilitate a national conversation about how we might respond to the challenges around childhood today, both as individuals and as a society. We want to promote a debate in which experts, policy makers, opinion formers, parents, carers, children and young people all have an important contribution to make.

The Unicef report and the Good Childhood Inquiry identify diverse factors that impact on children – from parents' working lives to play opportunities, from discrimination against young people to changing family structures. They point to a range of concerns in the lives of children and young people, among them an increase in depression, substance abuse and self-harm. We know that on some issues Wales

1

ranks worst in the UK – child poverty in particular is high. But there have also been a range of notable initiatives designed to improve the situation of children in Wales. The Welsh Assembly Government has embraced a Children's Rights framework in policy making. Wales was the first country in the UK to have a Children's Commissioner. The abandonment of Sats and league tables in schools, now proposed in England, took place here some years ago.

When we started thinking about this season in Summer 2008 we were fortunate in being able to draw on a significant body of work that had been produced by Funky Dragon over the previous two years, research which sought the views of children and young people. Among other things we took note of the resounding message that came through from children in the Why do People's Ages Go Up not Down? report of the crucial importance of play and play opportunities.

BBC Wales' audience is predominantly made up of adults and in posing the question *What are we doing to our kids?* we are asking that adults consider their responsibilities and agency in setting the framework that children and young people inhabit. We have all of course been children, so we also see an opportunity to draw on adult perspectives on the ways that childhood has changed. We thought that some new research could help us to do this so we talked to the Institute of Welsh Affairs about our emerging plans for the season. They proposed focus groups across three generations which provide the basis for the report that follows.

Though this research is modest in scale it is valuable in drawing attention to some trends and issues which are in a sense hiding 'in plain sight' but which warrant further consideration. Children place great value on talking and being listened to, by parents in particular. Though parents are keenly aware of this need they cite busy, stressful lives and work pressures as getting in the way of 'quality' time with their children. Parents and grandparents notice a greater confidence and articulateness in children now and parents say that the quality of communication they have with their children is an improvement on what they had with their own parents. These are positive notes in the report which provide a welcome counter to the worrying headlines that followed the Good Childhood Inquiry. On the negative side, all the parents and grandparents interviewed believe that children today have lost something that they felt was an important aspect of childhood – the freedom to go out and about and to play unsupervised at times. Some commentators will undoubtedly draw the conclusion that the media, including the BBC, need to take a fresh look at their own role in triggering the parental anxiety which contributes to this change.

We know that childhood, and the quality of opportunity offered to children in Wales is close to our audiences' hearts. This is evident in the transcripts of the focus groups and in the fact that, despite the busy lives they describe, the parents and grandparents who volunteered for the groups - who it is worth noting were mainly women - felt it was valuable to take the time to share their experiences and observations of parenting and childhood today.

Childhood is a complex business, and while there are some common themes across the focus groups the report underlines the fact that children's situations and experiences in Wales are diverse. In asking *What are we doing to our kids?* we should be aware that children and young people are both experts in the field and major stakeholders in the discussion. We need to listen closely to what they are telling us about their lives.

Finally I'd like to thank the children and adults who took part in the focus groups and welcome all those who want to take part in what we hope will be a stimulating and productive conversation.

Mandy Rose
Creative Director, Multiplatform
BBC Cymru Wales

Introduction

In a New Year interview at the end of 2008 the Children's Commissioner for Wales, Keith Towler, called for a national debate on how we are bringing up our children. Voicing fears that many children were suffering emotional deprivation in their relationship with their parents, he said there were three types of child poverty: financial, lack of opportunity, and the poverty of not being properly supported:

> *"It's the basics we are talking about here – being there for your child, setting boundaries, being responsible, giving love and guidance... It's about the simple things central to family life. How many families in Wales will be sitting down together to enjoy a family meal? Not very many. And how many of us have put on the TV, put our children in front of it and then said to our children, 'You watch that now, while I go and do something else'? We all do it. But it's when it's when done time after time after time that the real problems start. Significant numbers of adults are now routinely emotionally absent from their children."* [1]

It was a timely comment in relation to this BBC Wales-commissioned study which, by then, was well underway. Focus group interviews held across Wales in mid December 2008 had already captured some of the same concerns in comments made by parents themselves. There was a good deal of worry, especially amongst the working parents, that they were not spending sufficient 'quality time' with their children.

---

[1] *Western Mail*, 'Children's 'tsar' fears for quality of parenting in Wales', 27 December 2008.

However, it would be wrong to suggest that any of the adults we spoke with in the focus groups could be said to be 'emotionally absent' from their children or grandchildren. To the contrary, the fact that they volunteered to take part in the study suggests a strong concern.

And, indeed, this study picks up some highly positive features about today's children and their experiences of growing up in contemporary Wales. Children today are generally far more outgoing, confident and outspoken than their parents or grandparents were when they were young. For instance, they are far more likely to have open conversations with their parents on a basis of friendly equality about a wide range of issues. As the Children's Commissioner, who was a member of the Steering Group that advised this project, said at one of our meetings, commenting on a draft of this report, "If you take the trouble to listen there are fantastic things being said." And although there are concerns, especially about the greater restrictions placed on children these days in terms of their ability to roam and play unsupervised, at the same time they tend to have a much more varied range of experiences at an earlier age.

This IWA study examines children's experiences of growing up in Wales today from the perspective of three generations. Focus group conversations were undertaken with children aged 10-11 in three contrasting primary schools across Wales: in inner-city Cardiff; in the Valleys; and in a Welsh-medium primary school in north-east Wales. Focus group discussions were also held in the same locations with parents and carers, and also grandparents and other carers of the grandparents' generation. The objective was to record inter-generational views on family life and relationships, the nature of play and freedom to roam, boundaries and rules, and views about what the future holds for today's children. Among the questions explored with the focus groups were:

- *Do we spend enough time together as families? Do we eat together regularly?*
- *Do children and parents communicate freely? What are the areas of tension?*
- *How do children balance screen time and play time?*
- *Are our fears for children's safety denying them necessary opportunities for learning and developing independence? How far from home and at what age are children allowed to go unsupervised?*

The interviews were conducted with groups of around ten people, and each lasted about an hour. The discussions were recorded and transcribed and form the basis of this study. Discussions of this kind are a well-tried qualitative research method for engaging with relatively intimate and subjective themes. They allow for an in-depth exploration of the views of children, parents and grandparents in their own words and on their own terms. Although there are many examples of focus group work with children, it is unusual for views on themes of this kind to be captured simultaneously from three generations. We believe this provides a unique perspective on the issues explored and how views about them have changed over time. In addition, the interviews provide a very different insight from the largely quantitative picture shown in other recent studies that have explored broadly similar themes.[2]

At the same time it should be stressed that this is not a scientific survey. It is a snapshot of the views of nine small groups of people at a particular moment. The children who participated were selected by their teachers, and the parents and grandparents all volunteered in response to a circular invitation sent out on behalf of the IWA by the schools involved.

It should be noted too that, although the children's groups were evenly balanced between boys and girls, the adult groups were largely made up of women. This, perhaps, reflects their generally greater involvement with the upbringing of children. In Chapter 6, in which various experts offer a commentary on the findings, Catriona Williams, Chief Executive of Children in Wales, suggests that further work is needed to explore the reasons why fathers did not engage in the discussions to the same extent as mothers.

The IWA is extremely grateful to the schools and especially the headteachers for their ready co-operation without which the project

---

[2] See, for example: (i) UNICEF, Innocenti Research Centre, Report Card 7, 'An overview of child well-being in rich countries', Florence, February 2007; (ii) National Family and Parenting Institute Survey conducted by Mori, *Teenagers Attitudes to Parenting*, 2000, involving interviews with 2,343 children aged 11-16 from a representative sample of secondary and middle schools across England and Wales (237 from Wales) and separate interviews with 2,059 adults; and (iii) Funky Dragon, *Why do people's ages go up not down?* A Funky Dragon report asking to what extent are children aged 7 to 10 in Wales able to access their rights (as defined by the United Nations Convention on the Rights of the Child), 2007, www.funkydragon.org

could not have been undertaken. Appendix 1 provides outline profiles of the schools involved in the study, and Appendix 2 lists the members of the Steering Group which has advised the project. The report was discussed at a series of seminars during February 2009 at Llandudno, Aberystwyth, and Swansea. These engaged with people directly involved in work with children and young people. The report was also presented and discussed at a meeting in Bala with members of Funky Dragon's 100-strong Grand Council of 11-25 year olds.

John Osmond
Director, IWA

Chapter 1
Family Life and Relationships

Many children mentioned their desire to be listened to when they spoke about their relationships with loved ones, friends and teachers:

"I talk to my brother the most because he's the only one who just sits and talks to me."
Male pupil

"I talk to my brother 'cause he understands me, even though he is annoying."
Male pupil

"I am comfortable talking to teachers - because they listen to you."
Female pupil

Ensuring children receive attention seems to be a matter of opportunity, owing to the very busy lives of parents. Some parents mentioned travelling to and fro from school as a good time to 'just chat':

"They talk to you then. Sometimes it's easier when they're doing something else as well, like walking. They say more than if you sit them down and try and ask them things."
Female parent

"I find it a good time on the way home to say how did your day go? What did you do today? Anything good? Anything interesting?"
Female parent

And one pupil observed that her mother liked to talk about her day during the journey home:

"After school my mother in the car always asks the same question: How was school? What did you do in school?"
Female pupil

In most cases children seemed to pick whomever they felt most comfortable with to discuss different subjects at particular moments in time:

"I usually talk to my gran. She's the person I would talk to as I don't really like my mother."
Female pupil

"Say someone did something in school to me, like be racist or something, I would tell my mum and then my mum would just give me advice about things that you can do. She'd say just ignore the person, he – or she – just wants attention, to get you started and have a fight or get in trouble."
Male pupil

Trust was an important element to children's communication. They valued people whom they could trust and talk to about secrets and potentially embarrassing subjects:

"Say if I had a problem and I don't want to talk with mum I'll talk to my friends and ask them what they would do. They give me advice because I can trust them and they won't tell people."
Female pupil

"I like talking to dad because I tell him things and he tells me things. We keep it a secret."
Male pupil

"My mother was very open with me. I could ask her anything, which was good, and that's how I feel like I am with my little girl. I wouldn't want her to be scared to not come and ask me if she ever needed to. I hope I have I got that same relationship."
Female parent

9

This was true for other generations as well. In the Valleys location grandparents discussed who they had spoken with about problems when they were younger:

"A sister, if you had a sister; you wouldn't talk to your parents about it would you?"
Female grandparent

"Oh no, no, no."
Female grandparent

"Your friends, it would either be your friends - or if you had a sister or brother."
Female grandparent

Parents across the focus groups found difficulty in making opportunities for 'quality time' with their children, and knowing how to spend it. Marital status was a key determinant. As one parent put it:

"I'm separated from my partner, so I'm on my own now. I work all day and then have my kids all night. I can really empathise with the 24/7 idea. There's just no respite. I'm not the only one who is looking after their kids on their own. I know a lot of other people in the same boat. Looking back when I was growing up everyone was in couples. So I think that impacts on how much quality time you have with your kids."
Female parent

"I'm always rushed and prioritising time. It's quality time with them that I lack. Sometimes I have to think what is quality time these days. Is it taking them somewhere? It's not really, is it? It's doing nothing with your children, just talking to them, and listening to them."
Female parent

A grandfather from the north Wales commented:

"I'm old fashioned really. When my two grandchildren come round they have to sit at the table and try a knife and fork - but I realise how hard it is for my daughter to raise two young children on her own. Sometimes is hard to get discipline, but they're coming along."
Male grandparent

10

Difficulty in finding quality time was not confined to single or separated parents. Pursuing a career and the general hectic nature of their lives were cited by parents generally in the focus groups as potential obstacles to their spending time and being involved in their children's lives. A mother from the Cardiff school said:

"I'm lucky. I only work two days a week. It was a conscious decision to do that so I could spend time when the children were small. I've got friends that work full time and they are just constantly stressed about getting from work to make sure they spend enough time with the children. They feel guilty, so then they sign them up to all sorts of things, so I think I'm lucky in that sense."
Female parent

"I think sometimes the father in the situation - or sometimes it's the mother these days - has to work quite long hours and they come in late and they miss a lot of the children's childhood. My husband used to come in quite late, when the children were about 11 or 12. I very often had to go the parents' evenings on my own, because he was held up at work or he was working away, had to go abroad and that had an impact. He feels he missed out a lot on their childhood. I think that happens today too."
Female grandparent

"Because I worked when they were little, my parents looked after the kids a lot of the time. When they look back they're going to remember cooking with my mother, not with me. She did all the nice things with them."
Female parent

A mother from the Cardiff school contrasted the time her parents had for her, compared with her own busy life:

"Because my parents didn't work they had more time. I'm working full time, my husband's working and then my son goes to mosque. So by the time I finish from work and go home, they got to have something to eat quickly and then I got to drop them at the mosque at 5 o'clock. Then I've got to go and pick my little one and come home and do cooking while they are in the mosque. After that pick them up from the mosque at 7 o'clock. When they come home,

they'll have something to eat and that's the time we can have some fun. We try to have evening meals together. But still you never have enough time to go into deeper discussion. They get so tired you see. By then it's time for then to go bed, because they got to get up early, at 7 o'clock to come with me to school. So they have to be early. I find it is only weekends when you're trying to do something with them and you do feel guilty, like I'm not giving them enough time. I should be spending more time with them. When I was a child my parents were there all the time."
Female parent

A number of grandparents thought things had changed for the worse due to both parents being in full-time work:

"Parents today haven't got the time to spend with their children that we had."
Female grandparent

"I think they lose their patience with them."
Female grandparent

"She loses her patience very quickly. She's up to here with work when she comes home."
Female grandparent

"I think a lot of the pressure comes from parents who are working too much. With both parents in work they have very little time for the children. They're both educated parents, they've got high-flying jobs that they don't want to give up and the children don't have enough of their time. They have material things, plenty of material things, but they don't have time. They're not spoken to enough, they're not given enough experiences, they're not taken out enough. That has a detrimental effect on their wellbeing."
Female grandparent

"She doesn't feel that she's got the patience to deal with him. You know, she wants to give him time but having said that she has to spend some time in the evenings preparing for her work as a teacher. I wouldn't like her to hear this but I think she is impatient with him."
Female grandparent

"And the children are stressed out as well."
Female grandparent

All the grandparents in the Valleys school said they were closely involved in the day-to-day lives of their grandchildren. The same was true with some of the grandparents in the other schools, though not all. At the Cardiff school one grandparent said:

"I have a lot of involvement with my grandchildren. As much as I can 'cause they stay overnight. I take them to school some mornings and then I go to work. I work in the area, so it's good for me. I do a lot of things with them outside school."
Female grandparent

Grandparents in the Valleys described a close daily involvement with their grandchildren's upbringing:

"I see my grandchildren 7 days a week 8 hours a day, you know, when there's no school. You bring them to school and you pick them up to take them home and you feed them until their mother comes home from work. That's five days a week."
Female grandparent

"They spend really more time with their grandparents than they do with their parents"
Female grandparent

"The majority of the people fetching children after school here are grandparents."
Female grandparent

When asked if this was a positive thing these grandparents said they enjoyed it:

"I love it."
Female grandparent

"If you want to help your family you look after them, don't you?"
Female grandparent

Both parents and grandparents mentioned meal times as an ideal opportunity to spend time with the children. A few mentioned that they wanted to repeat their own childhood experiences of meal times. Generally meal times were very important to parents. As a Valleys mother put it:

"I think that's when we do most of our talking really because we are fortunate that we are all there at meal times together. We all eat the same meal and that's when we find out about each other's days. Not all families are that fortunate with work commitments and things. But for me its one meal one sitting, that's it."
Female parent

However, a north Wales mother described mealtimes as something of a struggle:

"I do try and structure our mealtimes, but some days I just feed the kids and I just sit with them but at least with tea I do try and sit us all at a table and eat as a family and talk about the day."
Female parent

Consciousness of the importance of mealtimes was widespread, as this Cardiff mother said:

"That's one thing I remember from my childhood. We always sat together for breakfast, lunch, and dinner. We always sat around and had a meal around the table, so we do that as well. We always have a Sunday roast on Sunday. That's something I remember from my childhood and we've got back to it now. I would say meal times are very important and also bed times. My children are just avid book readers. It's a time for winding down as well, about an hour before bed. I would say they are quite important times."
Female parent

However, many did not share meals this way, owing to practical difficulties or the unwillingness of family members to sit at a table. As one Valleys mother put it:

"I've had a battle for the last 10 years since they were born. Dinner time has been terrible because they just won't sit at the table. I'm just hoping that eventually they will learn to sit at the table properly."
Female parent

And a Cardiff grandmother observed:

"We used to have our meals on the table at teatime, and Sunday dinner and Sunday tea. We don't do that anymore. Most of the children I know don't do that anymore. It's trays on their lap in front of the TV."
Female grandparent

Some grandparents thought today's children were more aware of money than they had been when younger:

"We had little money in our day but we enjoyed our life."
Female grandparent

"I feel quite sorry for parents these days because there is a lot of financial pressure on them. I didn't have that with my children. When they were older, in their teens, and they went skiing once my daughter said: "Oh I don't want that jacket, I want a different one". Up until then when they were primary age they never looked at what other people had. Children never commented on having the right clothes."
Female grandparent

Parents tended to think there had been less of a change in this respect between their childhood and the experience of their children:

"As a child, if somebody had a pair of Adidas trainers, I'd say 'Well so and so has had Adidas trainers', so I think it hasn't changed much really."
Female parent

Generally, however, there was a perception that today's children were more aware of money matters. Parents and grandparents at the Cardiff Primary said there had been a change over generations:

"I've got two boys and they're just aware of everything. He's aware of mortgages, car insurance, you know. He's just soaking it up and it's around all time. You try and see what they're watching on TV but I'm not in there all the time. You know he was saying 'Go on mum, get a quote on the internet' for house insurance. I wasn't aware of finance and money in that way. I certainly didn't desire

money the way that my kids do. They're really aware and the ideas they have for Christmas presents – they want laptops and mobile phones when they're six or seven!"
Female parent

"I've noticed that with my boy and he's only seven. I had to tell him to stop asking people how much they earn."
Female parent

Shopping was raised by the children more than once. Although a few boys mentioned that they went to shops for themselves or on behalf of relatives none said they actually enjoyed going. However, in two of the focus groups girls mentioned shopping as a pastime, in the context of discussions about play and leisure time:

"I like brownies, basketball and shopping."
Female pupil

Another, in north-east Wales, mentioned that she looked forward to going shopping when older:

"I can see myself going shopping with my friends - to Cheshire Oaks or Chester or to Wrexham because I've never been there."
Female pupil

Pocket money arrangements varied from one household to another. Some children received pocket money regularly and others asked for things they wanted on an ad hoc basis:

"I don't get pocket money though sometimes dad gives me money to go on holiday."
Male pupil

"You just ask for money if you want something."
Female pupil

"If I see something I like then dad thinks about it."
Male pupil

"I don't have pocket money but if I want something I just beg my mother like please, I need it."

Female pupil

"I only get pocket money if I do something good for the family.
I ask my parents for money they say earn it first. So it's not really
like pocket money every week; I just get money for earning it."
Female pupil

"I only get pocket money if I wash the dishes or something like
that – doing house work that's the only time I ever get it."
Male pupil

The subject of identity and ethnicity was raised by children at the
Cardiff school, where about half of the pupils come from mixed
ethnic backgrounds. The children were fully aware of the subject,
but not so aware of differences:

"This kid in year 3 said to me 'No black people allowed' and I said
I was gonna knock him out, silly. I never though, I just ignored
him and told my mum and my mum came up the school."
Male pupil

"I think you're lying. He's black so why would he say
'No blacks allowed'?"
Male pupil

"He's not black, he's Asian."
Female pupil

It was acknowledged that some ethnic minority children had
difficulty integrating into school. These were mainly personal,
relationship difficulties:

"When you come here and learn people might make fun of you and
sometimes they'll help you, like be friends with you. Sometimes it
can be really hard to mix in with the rest of the English people.
You're really different compared from them."
Female pupil

"We're all the same. But in their minds, prejudiced people think
we're, like the enemy. But us, we just want to be friends."
Male pupil

Some of the children seemed to place teasing about ethnicity in the same category as jibes about other physical characteristics:

"Say like you're from a different country, some of us could be really kind to them and some of them will just talk about them behind their back."
Male pupil

"Like 'Look at her, she's black' or 'she's white' or something like that."
Female pupil

"She's so small."
Male pupil

"She's fat, she's ugly, she's big."
Male pupil

Pupils in the other focus groups were more aware of gender and generally had strong opinions on differences between boys and girls. In the north-east Wales school there was no consensus and there seemed to be no answer to whether the children themselves talked differently with each other depending on whether they were boys or girls. In the Valleys school, however, there was a clearer awareness of such differences:

"Boys are silly."
Female pupil

"You wouldn't talk to a boy about a problem you have. Unless it's an 'everyone' problem, but definitely not a boy problem."
Female pupil

"Some of the girls are like in to High School Musical and they support different football teams. If you're talking about football and you say the team you support, they say a different team just because they like Cristiano Ronaldo or Wayne Rooney or something like that."
Male pupil

"Girls talk gossip and spread it."
Female pupil

"I don't talk to girls that much 'cause when you tell 'em stuff they always spread it round the school."
Male pupil

Chapter 2

Play and Freedom

As a prompt to discussion the children were asked to draw, within a graphical representation of the home, their favourite indoor activities, and on a blank sheet their favourite activities outside the house.

The Valleys children made it clear that technological devices have an important influence on their experience of play time inside the house. Items and activities referred to included television, computer games, Nintendo DS, PS2, listening to music, telephones, laptops, and games consoles such as Xbox 360, and playstations, although pets and musical instruments also featured. However, when asked to depict their favourite place to play, none of the Valleys children referred to the activities they had drawn inside the house. In fact, they mentioned completely different things. These now included mountains, a football pitch, streets, back gardens, and parks. One child said:

"I like going to choir practice as they've got a big field and we can have a run around before we go in."
Male pupil

This pattern was largely repeated with children in the other focus group locations. They enjoyed technology-related games but also activities outside the house as well. One of the Cardiff children said:

"Inside I've drawn a TV because I like playing all my games on the TV – and most of all watching TV. Outside I have done a football,

because I like to play sports outside."
Male pupil

A child from north-east Wales commented:

"Well, I like playing in the park mostly, playing football or netball, and I like taking the dog and playing things like tag and hide and seek."
Male pupil

While a Valleys child added:

"It's better when you can go out to play than when you're stuck inside on a nice day. It's not very nice."
Male child

The main shift between the generations in the field of play seemed to be a reduction in free play and an increase in participation in organised activities. As a Valleys parent, said, reflecting on the changes:

"Our children are able to go to all these music classes and do all the sports and things, that we wouldn't do. They all cost money and there's no way my parents would have paid for me to go somewhere different every night. So in one way we benefited from the freedom aspect but then they're benefiting from leaving school and having all these swimming awards and the choices."
Female parent

Some children enjoyed doing different activities, while others did not always enjoy it. One Valleys girl said:

"I like the weekdays the best because on the weekends it's normally 'pants'. On the weekdays I have Brownies and different stuff to do."
Female pupil

A Cardiff boy said:

"Sometimes my friends can't go out and sometimes I have to go to clubs and things. I like going to them but I'd rather go out and play sometimes."
Male pupil

Asked to describe his favourite time one north-east Wales boy said he liked being alone:

"When my mum and sister are working. Sometimes I like to be on my own."
Male pupil

A few children mentioned traditional activities and games or spontaneous activities that they liked and which stimulated their imagination:

"Sometimes I play with people, well with Barbie. I like to do adventures with my Barbie. They go swimming, camping and climb small trees and they live in a boarding school."
Female pupil

"Inside, we like to play touch the ceiling. What we do is we try to touch the ceiling and then we jump on the chairs trying to touch it."
Female pupil

"I normally play football out the yard or you can just make up a game otherwise."
Male pupil

When asked to think about their abiding memories and the best thing about their own childhood the responses from almost all the adults were very similar:

"I think the best part of being a child was the freedom. You played in the street for hours or you went up the mountain for a picnic, whereas I find now I've got a nine year old little girl and unless she's got somebody's house to specifically be going to or a club you're very reluctant to say 'just go out and wander about'. I think most of her time would be spent going to different clubs or somebody else's house rather than just playing in the street but streets are far busier now than they were when I was a child."
Female parent

"My memory is the freedom that we had as children compared to children today. We were free to have a few jam sandwiches and a home made bottle of squash and we went up the mountain for

picnics, pretend games and make believe games. We thoroughly enjoyed the freedom of play that children today haven't got. Nobody was panicking where we were because they knew where and they knew we would be safe. There were nowhere near as many organisations that children have got now to go to but they were better attended then because there weren't so many places to go. We had fun."
Female grandparent

"I suppose the big one for me is playing out locally, going to the local mountaineers' children and having rope swings and going out on bikes and feeling safe doing it. Just saying to my mum I'm just popping there, they knew where we were, we knew where they were. We played with simple things like a rope swing; we had a lot of joy and pleasure out of it."
Female parent

At the Cardiff Primary school one parent recalled a childhood in rural Pakistan and how the move to urban south Wales brought social and geographic changes that militated against the children going out more to play:

"Quite happy memories actually, which I do feel my children are missing out because when it's in the countryside you can go out freely, you know your neighbours, and everybody. Over here they can't do that. They can't go out to play. So they are missing out on that."
Female parent

However, not all the adults at the school perceived so many changes:

"I don't see much differences really apart from the computers they have now which I never had, and the mobile phones. When my grandchildren come to stay I still do the same things that my mum and my dad used to do with us."
Female grandparent

Overall, however, there was a strong and repeatedly expressed feeling that children's lives now are more organised and supervised by adults. The focus groups were asked to consider why children tended to play in the manner they did. Very few parents – and none in Cardiff –

said they gave their children the same free rein to play and roam in their locality that they had. Danger from strangers was the children's most commonly cited reason for restrictions on their freedom.

The children in north-east Wales seemed to be offered the most freedom, possibly because it is located in a semi-rural area. The following exchange shows this, an atypical example when compared with the children from the Valleys and Cardiff schools:

"I can go from my house to Buckley because my Nan lives right by there. Sometimes I walk, sometimes I go on my bike."
Male pupil

"My mum doesn't really mind. If it's just me on my own I'll stay in a place that I know because I don't want to go to somewhere strange because I just tend to walk on my own to friends' houses."
Female pupil

In the Valleys and Cardiff, however, children tended to be given lifts or escorted on foot to take part in activities or go to friends' houses. Some children were allowed to play and roam, but with limitations. These included being accompanied by siblings or taking a mobile telephone to ensure they could be contacted.

Parents and grandparents varied in their concern about the extent of perceived threats to children when they were outside the home. Traffic and parked cars featured highly in their minds. In addition, a significant number of respondents were conscious of 'stranger danger'. One Cardiff parent complimented the children's ability to understand the danger posed by people they did not know:

"They're quite good at knowing about stranger danger."
Female parent

The children themselves had clear ideas about the potential dangers that faced them as they played or moved around in public spaces. In north-east Wales one boy said:

"You're very safe in the house but outside even if you're comfortable with the place you still don't know if someone's going to jump out at you."
Male pupil

Without any prompting children in the Cardiff Primary used graphic terms to describe the potential dangers. Asked why they were not allowed out on their own the children responded:

"If you get kidnapped; or a man takes you, or a woman."
Female pupil

"There is a man going around and he is a proper paedophile. He goes around in a white van, saying "Would you like a lift?" And he takes them back to his place and kidnaps and kills them. And rapes them and does everything... bad things to them."[3]
Female pupil

"I'm not allowed to go out really because my mum worries about me a lot even with the whole family. If we stay out a bit too long she worries and she goes really crazy and she goes outside trying to look for us, so that's why I normally have to go outside with my dad or with my mum."
Female pupil

"Sometimes your parents may go off on one with you but then you're still their child and they love you, so they just get worried."
Female pupil

In the Valleys school the children's fears were more specific and tended to be focused on localities to avoid, referring for example to perceived dangers elsewhere:

"I wouldn't go as far as [the next town down the Valley] 'cause it is where they drink on the streets and kick me, and just come up to me. They just come up for a chat. You don't know them; they talk to strangers."
Female pupil

"I'd never go to [another town in the Valley]. There are a lot of pubs there."
Male pupil

---

[3] Some months earlier, prompted by the police, a number of Cardiff inner-city primary schools had circulated a note to parents alerting them to a white van that had been noticed on a number of occasions outside a school.

"Yeah, it's scary."
  Male pupil

Asked about the problem with pubs another Valleys child responded:

"People could come out of there drunk, alcoholics, and like they
  could just grab you, have a go at you."
  Male pupil

Other children in the same focus group had experienced trouble
from older children and teenagers while playing:

"Well, usually up the park where I live: you have people there,
  stupid people always drinking. When you go up there and you play
  football they just nick your ball and boot it away. I seen a boy
  who's 12 and I seen him smoking."
  Male pupil

One child at the north-east Wales school suggested that he became
scared of his own accord, while acting on parental instructions to
go out alone:

"Sometimes I cycle to the town to get shopping for mum but
  sometimes I get scared just before the town and come back."
  Male pupil

Other children were less inclined to be cautious and actually enjoyed
going against parental instructions in a spirit of childhood rebellion:

"There are rules but I usually don't listen to her because I like going
  up mountains. She says 'you can't go up the mountains today it's
  too wet,' so I just go up anyway. If she says you can go up the
  mountain I usually go somewhere else."
  Male pupil

Parents struggled with the dilemma of keeping their children safe from
harm while allowing them a healthy level of freedom and free play to
develop. Parents in the Valleys school summed up the feelings many have:

"In my opinion I don't think it's safe, you know, to go out and play."
  Female parent

"We don't know where the paedophiles are. They won't tell us, so it's fear of who might be there in our community."
Female parent

On the other hand a few felt guilty that they tended towards restriction rather than freedom:

"My fear is someone will do them some harm, although I also think I should be giving them freedom. I should be letting them out more. But I'm sure the roads are the worst danger but perhaps I'm being irrational."
Female parent

"Today's children have lost their freedom. When I was growing up we had the opportunity to go out and find our own things and learn things ourselves but today parents keep them in sight and they don't get the chance to learn for themselves."
Male parent

Some thought the nature of the threat from strangers had changed:

"I mean dirty old men were only that when we were young - they'd just expose themselves. Now they want children."
Female grandparent

Media coverage of dangers to children was frequently cited. The media had the potential to exaggerate dangers, according to both parents and grandparents. Some thought that it was the awareness of dangers that had changed rather than the true reality and drew attention to the role of the media:

"There were dangers years ago too. I think that the papers and the media create more scares in hearts of parents."
Male parent

"It's always been the same. There's always been children disappearing."
Female parent

"The media report a lot more of it and it gets highlighted."
Female parent

A Cardiff mother contrasted the contemporary situation with a generation ago:

"Today we have to bear the pain of the world, you know. Our parents, it was just the people they knew, but now it's everything: one disaster after another. Every child and we have to take all that on-board and in a way that makes it very difficult to feel safe."
Female parent

"I think when the Madeline McCann thing happened the children were so aware of it but you want to protect them from having to worry about being afraid of strangers. It's drawing a fine line, I think."
Female parent

"Now children are so aware of what's going on in the media with newspapers and my daughter will come and say that she's heard of what's happened and she will ask questions and it's drummed into them. I'm paranoid about safety."
Female parent

A father from north Wales thought media coverage was stifling children's development:

"There is a change. There's a change in society from the media. You have got to watch children more but I think as a society – I may be wrong - we've become overprotective. I do get annoyed. It goes back to risk; if you're never allowed to appreciate risk and become involved with risk how can you evaluate the risk? If you're constantly protected then you think you'll always be safe. And, of course, you're not because one day you'll be somewhere facing something and you won't be able to assess that risk. I do think we've gone too far simply because of that."
Male parent

According to focus group participants in Cardiff, neighbourhoods had changed. Communities no longer looked out for children in the way they did:

"I do think it's true that years ago the general community looked out for kids or looked after kids a bit more than they do now. Other adults would feel free to tell somebody else's children off."
Female parent

A grandparent, also in Cardiff, made a similar point about community engagement:

"If your mum was a bit late, you could always go into your neighbour's house, they would feed you and look after you. We had a lot of freedom and yet we were still warned about dangers in our daily life and in school. We always had somebody looking after us in the street. Neighbours were all families and they had lived there for a long time. Once you lived there in the house you never moved. You weren't on the move like they are now. So you got to know your family and neighbours and they looked after you. Now it's a lot different. Sometimes you could be in the street for years and you don't even know some neighbours moved in next door. We had a lot more freedom but we were still had a lot of dangers that we looked out for too."
Female grandparent

However a child in north Wales testified to a contemporary experience of neighbourhood involvement still:

"When I go home I'm okay for a bit. But one evening I had gone home and I thought my brother and sister would have come straight home. My sister didn't get home until 4:30 and I had been home for an hour, so now if no one's home after half an hour I go next door or over the road."
Female pupil

Roads seemed a particular problem for the parents and grandparents of the south Wales schools, and in particular the Primary in Cardiff which is bounded by a number of busy shopping and residential streets:

"If people drove more sensibly it would be a bit better. The volume of traffic is not the only problem, it's the way people drive as well. That's a big one for parents I think."
Female grandparent

"You can teach them how to cross a road and let them do it when you're there. But when they've got to go on there own you gotta remember the height of them, they can't see past parked vans."
Female parent

"It's the speed of the cars coming through the street that stops me letting them out more. Everyone is in such a rush; they are just speeding through the street."
Female parent

The accompaniment of an older sibling was a precondition for some children to play outside the house:

"I'm allowed to go most places with my brother but not on my own."
Male pupil

Parents were also conscious that the peers who accompanied their children were important:

"I think as well it's the luck of the child they go out with as well, if you know they are going out with a child that's on the same wavelength."
Female parent

The varying rates of children's development also seemed a consideration for parents and grandparents. When considering the age at which a child would be allowed to play more freely the child's individual circumstances and character were considered important.

"I think it's the way your children react with you and their common sense levels."
Female grandparent

"My daughter's been asking to walk to school. She goes to the shops and I might even consider letting her walk to school, but not her little brother, who's a complete menace on the roads."
Female parent

"I think the amount of licence you allow your grandchildren or children really depends on the child. I mean one of my grandchildren I would have no difficulty at all in allowing him to go down from town to my house but the other one, who likes running everywhere, I have to sit him down and tell him that it's dangerous."
Male grandparent

One Valleys parent was concerned that the pattern of children's play and leisure time was preventing them developing independence:

"I've got to take them to somebody's house, pick them up or they go to something after school or in the evenings. In a sense that's taking their independence away from them because we were responsible for our play when we were kids. We would just decide what we got up to in the school holidays without our parents organising it."
Female parent

At the Cardiff Primary the children were asked at what age they would need to be before being let out alone:

"Eighteen."
Male pupil

"Twelve."
Female pupil

"My sister is 17 and still my mum worries about her, and says not to go out and come back really late unless she's with a grown up. So when I'm fully an adult."
Female pupil

"Sixteen, seventeen or eighteen."
Male pupil

"In America you're not allowed to drink until you're 21!"
Male pupil

As would be expected, location played a large part in determining children's play. Pupils attending a school from widely scattered households experienced less local and often more informal play. This was the case at the north-east Wales Primary, which like many Welsh-medium schools has a relatively wide catchment area, extending beyond the immediate urban environs into a rural hinterland:

"The fact that I've chosen that they go to a Welsh speaking school means they don't go to the school where all their friends are, so again their friends are spread all over. Often, if they want to go and play with their friends it's a case of taking them to their friends' houses."
Male parent

However, parents in Cardiff and the Valleys commented that despite living near their school the children were not very familiar with their neighbourhoods and the people who live in them. As one Cardiff parent put it:

"When I was growing up, I had friends living two or three doors down so we just called for each other and played. Whereas, I dunno, it seems to be spread out a lot more now. When I was young I had three or four friends who lived close by and I'd walk to their houses. I'd walk down the high street to my friends' houses, whereas they can't do that. Also, there are like four primary schools here that the children can go to. So they might be children quite close but they go to a different school."
Female parent

A Valleys mother recalled:

"We would know lots of people from all the streets around whereas I think my children don't know their community like that."
Female parent

Both parents and grandparents felt a greater need to keep watch over their children and grandchildren, or at least know exactly where they were:

"My kids – one, three and five – play in the garden, which I class as being quite safe. I'm pottering in the kitchen and I can see them on and off so I'm happy. Because my eldest is five I really have no idea in this day and age when I will let her out of my sight, or when I will allow her to go on the road or knock on next door."
Female parent

The advent of cheaper mobile telephones represents a significant technological change between today's young generation and their parents and grandparents. The most obvious advantage for parents is that it allows them to keep tabs on their children remotely – and also serves as an emergency tool. In the Valleys especially, where a few children mentioned that they liked to roam the mountains and hills, children and their parents talked about mobile phones in this way:

"I think it's peace of mind for the child and the parents though.

Knowing that if they do get into trouble or they get lost or something, they can phone you. You can be looking at the clock, thinking you haven't spoken to him now for three hours maybe but you can just ring him to check they're okay. So it's peace of mind really isn't it?"
Female parent

"If I take my mobile with me I tell my mother 'if you want me just phone me and I'll come back'."
Male pupil

One adult at the north-east Wales school mentioned the need for mobile phones as an alternative to phone boxes:

"I think the mobile phone is very good and handy because there are fewer and fewer phone boxes around to use as an emergency phone or to call and say 'Mum come and get me' or 'Mum I've finished whatever in the park'."
Male grandparent

In Cardiff, where parents and grandparents did not seem to often let their children roam, fewer children had mobiles. One parent commented:

"Mine would lose them; half a day and they'd lose them."
Female parent

Another parent agreed that mobiles were useful to watch over children but said that their children were not yet old enough:

"Once they get to high school they might be a lot further away from home. There might be issues with buses and missing lessons and things, so it's practical then."
Female parent

One grandparent had worries about the mobile phone's alleged health risks:

"We hear about the dangers of the masts but you need a stronger signal to transmit the message than receive it and kids are walking around with them held against their ears and that's right next to the brain."
Male grandparent

Others identified increased frequency of contact brought by mobiles which, they thought, could be problematic:

"When our own children went out to play we didn't have to worry about keeping in touch with them because we knew they would be safe, wherever they were."
Female grandparent

"To be honest you can't win with mobile phones. Years ago we didn't have them and my mum would think I was safe, whereas now if a child doesn't ring you…"
Female parent

Despite instant communication there were times when parents could not always instantly come to their children's aid, as one Valleys mother recalled:

"I bought my ten-year-old a phone when he was eight to keep an eye on him. I'm glad I did because he went up the mountain with his friends and got stuck up there. He phoned me on the mobile and said: "Can you get the helicopter for me?" I said: 'No, you can find your own way down. You got up there, you get down.' My other little boy was three at the time and there was no way I could go up the mountain with a three year old. Eventually he did come down the mountain. It was only Pentre mountain, you know, but I grounded him for going up it without telling me. He was crying going home and he cried the rest of day as well. He doesn't go up the mountain now unless we are with him. But all the same that was a good lesson because he eventually got down to the main road on his own."
Female parent

Chapter 3

Boundaries and Rules

The focus groups were asked to consider the rules and boundaries in children's lives. Who makes them? How are they enforced? What sanctions are available when they are not observed? A key issue for focus group participants was responsibility for standards of behaviour. Grandparents in particular seemed to think there had been a generational change among some families:

"It's not true of all families but in general I think behaviour and standards are definitely lower. It's what your expectations really are. Some parental expectations are not good and they don't correct bad behaviour. Children think that if they get into trouble their parents will question the school. They never blame the child; it can never be their child. It's always somebody else's fault."
Female grandparent

One adult participant, who is also a teacher, said that sometimes teachers found themselves combating a child's behaviour which was a consequence of parental choices at home:

"It's hard when they first come to school because a lot of children have never heard the word 'no'. They demand more attention from the class teachers and the teaching assistants. They have a lack of concentration, because they're not used to sitting down and doing things like playing games. They flit from one thing to another; they don't concentrate. They watch the television a lot, which they're glued too."

Female grandparent

Some adult respondents were convinced that the behaviour of some children mirrored a more general decline in public behaviour:

"Common courtesy has gone down hill in general among adults and children. Simple things like opening a door for someone, or offering a seat on the bus don't happen. Even respect whilst driving: if you stop to let a car past they don't even say thank you."
Male parent

"Discipline has become too lapsed now. As recently as last night I was coming home from the Shotton area and passed a number of people without lights on their bicycles. Well, it's a vehicle and it should have lights on. Discipline is courtesy and respect; if you want respect you must give respect and I think discipline comes in this way."
Male grandparent

Children in the focus groups had clear memories of being reprimanded:

"I get shouted at by mum and dad."
Female pupil

"I fall out with my mother if I go to bed a bit later than I usually do and I don't get up in the morning and I can't get up."
Female pupil

"Yeah! Yeah! She's shouting get up and she's always like 'you should go to bed earlier!'"
Female pupil

In contrast to other pupils a few children from ethnic minority backgrounds mentioned parental love and care as a motivation for discipline, as with these Cardiff girls:

"My mum only says she is strict because of my future. So, if I'm watching too much TV she'll say 'do your homework'. I have to listen to her 'cause it's for my future. It's for my life, my future, the way I'm gonna grow up. I have to be capable to do things on my own

when I grow up, so I have to learn from mum while I'm at home."
Female pupil

"It's important not to watch too much TV, because if you watch too much you'll be unhealthy. Parents do so much for you and you don't even notice."
Female pupil

A number of parents and grandparents emphasised the importance of structure and routine in children's lives:

"I think routine is more important than rules."
Female parent

"Parents tend to treat their kids as a young adults these days. If they want to go out they just take them with them. There's no routine in their lives."
Female grandparent

"If they have a late night usually it does tell in the morning."
Female parent

Most of the children in the focus groups said they took opportunities to break out of – or test – the structures in their lives:

"My father sometimes goes off to bed and I stay up for an extra two hours!"
Male pupil

"Once, mam said to me not to eat a lot of sweets so I went to the kitchen and ate most of the sweets."
Male pupil

"Sometimes, I like watching TV or playing on the computer and my mam tells me it's time to go to bed. I'm like 'oh five more minutes' and she's like 'no, you got to go now!'"
Male pupil

Sometimes breaking or testing rules was unintentional:

"I don't really do homework, 'cause I always lose it. I always put it

in my pocket and when I get home it's always gone. I can never find it. I'm always getting detention."
Male pupil

Some children were either able to exploit differences between parents, or grandparents in the application of rules and boundaries or simply experienced varying boundaries:

"I like the rules with my father around 'cause he'll just let you get anything from the shelves but with my mother like if you take your shoes up the stairs you have half your pocket money taken off you or something like that."
Female pupil

"Well, my daughter makes them and my oldest granddaughter tries to come to me to break them for her."
Female grandparent

"She just says no more television. My dad lets me but not my mam."
Male pupil

Parents and grandparents across the focus groups thought negotiation on some matters was important to ensure that children were treated fairly:

"I think you got to be flexible, you got to treat them as individuals as well. I think they do feel a bit special when they have got the ability to make some decisions for themselves but you have to be sensible as well."
Female parent

"I know with my girls they don't always agree with the boundaries I put in place. I'm sure my daughter would love to sit at the computer on MSN until 2 o'clock. But we discuss these things and I think they understand the rules. On the other hand when I was growing it was just like do it and don't question it, which almost makes you push the boundaries."
Female parent

"I think much of it's in the art of negotiation. Even though two of my kids are only three and five years old they are very clever at it. I would say they know the boundaries and the rules and they know what

they are and aren't allowed to do. Obviously they are children so they like to push me and their dad as far as they can. It's bed time and they've watched two Peppa Pig episodes and they're on their third, so do you really let them watch the end of it or do you negotiate and pause it before breakfast in the morning or negotiate a story instead?"
Female parent

"Our biggest problem now is that our granddaughter thinks she is the only child who's not allowed to go out on her own. She's nine. She walks to school with a friend, the friend comes and calls for her and they haven't got far to come. That's the most we let her do on her own because there's so many things going on around."
Female grandparent

"My oldest one will say to me: 'Why have I got to be back in by half past four when the others haven't got to be in by half past five?' My attitude is that it's dark, and I don't want them out when it's dark."
Female parent

However, some of the children did not think they had a chance to debate or discuss the rules, as the following children testified, the first two from the Valleys and the third from north Wales:

"My mother says if you don't like the rules you can't live in my house."
Female pupil

"My mother says 'My roof, my rules'."
Male pupil

"There's no discussion about rules in our house."
Male pupil

None of the parents and grandparents admitted to using smacking as a punishment:

"If I was naughty I'd get smacked. You can't smack your children now, or you're not supposed to."
Female grandparent

"I wouldn't dream now of touching my grandson."
Female grandparent

Sending children to their rooms or removing enjoyable activities have replaced smacking as a form of punishment:

"They don't get physically punished today so much. They just get privileges taken from them."
Male grandparent

"We've made a conscious decision and we've told them they'll never get hit. We've said that to them and they've never been and we won't. They know there's not gonna be any kind of punishment like that. So you know, it's like time out somewhere, sitting somewhere where there's nothing to do. Sending them upstairs could be actually might be quite enjoyable so it's finding something that they won't like. Television is the key with mine 'cause they love watching it and I have to limit them really, taking away something that they like doing."
Female parent

Many parents in the focus groups said they felt that social pressures and other matters out of their control were influencing the behaviour of their children. However, one participant, who was also a teacher, described how some parents were not taking responsibility for the children's behaviour:

"I don't think there's enough respect from the parents half the time. It's not just the children. The children get it from the parents. If there's an issue, very often the parents will say: 'Well who else did it? It wasn't their fault; it must have been somebody else's fault'. And they say all these things in front of the children, questioning your authority. And then the children have got no respect for the teachers either, so it comes mainly from that generation, I think, from the parent's generation."
Female grandparent

Swearing was one area of behaviour where grandparents thought there had been a change for the worse over time, with children more exposed to swearing by adults:

"I work in a park area and I hear swearing all the time in the park. Little children swearing, and their mothers! They swear back to them."
Female grandparent

"You didn't hear it like children today are hearing it from every adult and, if they are up a bit later, on the telly."
Female grandparent

"We were in a cafe earlier today having food – me and my friend – and this young couple came in with two children. They were sitting two tables away from us with two young babies and it was 'effing this' and 'effing that'."
Female grandparent

Many adults in the focus groups highlighted a lack of deference from children compared with their day:

"In my times the teachers were respected and treated as something different. I work in a school and when it comes to talking to the teachers, I get tongue tied because they're teachers. My grandchildren say: 'Oh look there's so and so there. Don't like him, or don't like her'. I find the attitude is totally different."
Female grandparent

"When I was small I tended to ask my friends questions rather than ask my parents. It was a different sort of relationship to what I've got with my children."
Female parent

"It was more formal then. You didn't call your parents' friends by name. You were in big trouble if you said that. They were aunties or uncles. I can remember as a child you could only address an adult as either mum or dad, grandma or aunty or uncle. I can remember being very puzzled by that. I never put that restraint on my children. And even so, we get told off sometimes for letting my children call people by their first names. I say 'You ask an adult what it is they want to be called'. But now there doesn't seem to be that formality anymore."
Female parent

"My daughter can say more things with me then I could say to my mum. There's more openness. There's a lot more openness when you talk to children. My grandchildren say things to me that I wouldn't dare say to my mother, certainly not my grandmother."
Female grandparent

"Sex education is a typical example. My parents never talked to me about things like that. I've got a quite young one and I've got a more or less grown up one too. The older two saw me having this baby, carrying a baby, so it was an ideal opportunity. I don't think my parents would ever talk to me about things like that."
Female parent

A few parents thought that this was a good thing. Together with the greater reasoning over discipline and rules, it showed that children were being treated with greater respect:

"Thirty years ago it wasn't considered that a child could have an opinion. Children were kind of a different species or they weren't quite human – a little subhuman. My parents would say: 'Oh, don't be silly, you can't have a headache'. Children behaved that way and it wasn't convenient for them. They were good parents and I had a happy childhood. But you were a child. You came in and you were told what to do by your mum or your dad unless you wanted to get into real trouble. I came from a family that still smacked."
Female parent

"I think children are often seen to be cheeky today when really they are just more assertive a lot of the time. They say what they are thinking."
Female grandparent

Children have become more confident thanks to the style of schooling, according to a few parents and grandparents:

"My children are a lot more confident than I was when I was their age. That's down to what they do in school. They're encouraged to speak in front of a group, whereas I would have died. It doesn't faze them at all. I think that's wonderful for when they're older."
Female parent

"I think it's very good that they are brought up to be confident. My husband's an example. When he started his working life and he had to take meetings or chair meetings he used to get into a dreadful state because he hated to speak in public. I think partly it was because he was never allowed to do that in school. And he always said to me that it's great in school that the children get up on the

stage and take assemblies, speak to the parents and speak in public. They get used to that and I think that's a very good thing that they do in school these days because children are more confident. We never did that when I was in school and I always found it very difficult to speak in public. Also, the way they are taught in school is different. When I was in school I can remember trying to hide my head when it was my turn to read because I hated to read out to the whole class. But teachers never ever do that now. That's not the way you teach them, you teach them to boost their confidence. And education has moved on a long way I think in primary schools, and that's why they're more confident."
Female grandparent

"My children are more confident. I wasn't that confident at that age. I would definitely swap that. I would like to have been that confident."
Female parent

Alongside these observations, parents and grandparents noticed a blurring between childhood and adulthood. Generally they were worried that children were taking part in activities normally associated with older people:

"Twelve-year-olds go to Cardiff in limousines, now, to clubs, dancing, don't they? You know, it's frightening I mean my granddaughter has gone twice on birthday parties and a parent has also gone but I mean they are in a room where only they can be. It's still worrying to think at that age they want to be doing things like that. I never did anything like that until I was about 20."
Female grandparent

"You know all the programs on TV – Bratz and Barbie – I used to hate Barbie but I prefer Barbie to Bratz. Because they're just made up with these huge eyes and little curvy figures and all that make up. The amount of advertising during children's TV. It's just thrown at them the whole time."
Female parent

"I think the children are growing up too fast mind. I think they are trying to keep ahead of what's going on. If somebody's got one thing somebody else wants it. I think they want to be as grown up as everybody else, whereas when I was little it was like 'don't be

growing up too quickly' now."
Female parent

"Today the kids have a different outlook on life haven't they? My granddaughter is twelve but she thinks she's older than 20 sometimes."
Female grandparent

Chapter 4
The Future

Transition to secondary school represented a very significant forthcoming milestone for many of the children. The perception of what this change would bring varied between the focus group locations. Worries included managing among older, often larger, children, the anticipated difficulty of schoolwork and making friends in new surroundings. Boys in particular were worried about bullying and encountering older children, as these comments, in turn from the Valleys, north Wales and Cardiff testify:

"I'm worried that I'm going to get bullied because my favourite lesson is science. I might get beat up and if I tell the teacher I might get beat up even more."
Male pupil

"I am frightened of being bullied."
Male pupil

"I'm scared they might make fun of me."
Male pupil

When asked how they might deal with bullying, or similar situations, the children had mixed reactions. At the Cardiff Primary the children were determined to respond to attempts to bully them, as the following exchanges indicate:

"If someone be nasty to me, I'll just be rude back."

Female pupil

"Beat the crap out of them."
Male pupil

"You will get in trouble but at least it's over and done with, like you give them what they deserved."
Female pupil

"You shouldn't fight back; you should have peace with yourself."
Male pupil

Children with older siblings were hopeful that their family connections would be helpful:

"I hope it won't be that bad because my brother's there."
Male pupil

"I am looking forward to going up, 'cause I know a lot of friends and cousins and all that, so then I'm just cool."
Female pupil

In the Valleys school there was a mixture of resignation and determination to make the best of a bad situation:

"I'll just have to cope really 'cause I don't really want to go."
Male pupil

"The only thing we can do is think positive and make new friends and try hard and do your best."
Female pupil

Generally, the girls raised the subject of making friends more than boys:

"You got to make new friends so it's quite hard."
Female pupil

"I'm looking forward to it because my best friend moved from here to [a Welsh-medium comprehensive school] and I couldn't stop crying and I'm looking forward to seeing her."
Female pupil

Other children were excited about novel aspects of secondary school:

"I'm a little bit excited because they have labs and experiments and things."
Female pupil

Parents and grandparents were more positive on the whole towards the move to secondary school, especially compared with concerns about the children's growing older more generally. Many parents – and a few grandparents - across the focus group locations referred to the greater support that children receive today:

"There's a lot more support these days for transition from when I went."
Female parent

"Yes, we'd just turn up on the first day and it was terrifying!"
Female parent

"I think schools try and do something more about it today. When I went I don't ever remember going to visit the school before I went there. When you went there the first day that was it. But these days the Year Six children do a lot. They visit the school and they have lessons with some of the teachers. They are given buddies among the older children to help them find their way around the bigger buildings. There's a lot more emphasis on the transition. They are given a lot more help these days."
Female grandparent

However, some grandparents saw worries about the move to secondary school as just another case of fear of the unknown. They seemed to think the challenges facing children moving schools had not changed fundamentally:

"I think it's the fear of the unknown with everything, isn't it?"
Female grandparent

"Yeah, you got this thing in your head until you're actually there and doing something."
Female grandparent

46

"It's still the same. It's still the same apprehension and everything else that we went through."
Female grandparent

Some had specific worries about transitional difficulties:

"They are in this school and they are in the same classroom all day. Then they go over there and they are in about seven different classrooms in the morning. My granddaughter's worry was about getting lost."
Female grandparent

"Where I was brought up I went to an all-girls school, which I wouldn't force upon them. It was very small with one form entry each year. So it was 250 children from Year Seven up to Year 12. Now they're faced with going to a massive comprehensive school. I know all of them are going and they've got to go but I'm not looking forward to it. There are so many schools and they're suddenly split up from their little friends groups, going into a huge school, with thousands."
Female parent

Those parents who had a choice about secondary schools their children could attend did not relish the opportunity, as these Cardiff parents attested:

"Round here there are so many schools, people spread all over the place. It's this issue of choice. I don't want choice, I just want the local school to be good and for them to go there. I don't want to suddenly discover religion and have to send them somewhere else, which a lot of people do."
Female parent

"There are choices you shouldn't have to make, aren't there?"
Female parent

Between generations there were consistently contrasting attitudes about the children's upcoming teenage years. The majority of children were generally positive about growing into the teenage years, which they said would bring greater freedom. As one Cardiff girl said:

"When you're a teenager you get more freedom. My parents tell me I'm not old enough yet to go out. We'll be able to go, like, clubbing and stuff."
Female pupil

Others looked forward to getting jobs or studying:

"I want to go to college 'cause I know I can get quite a good job and things. I want to be a singer when I'm older."
Female pupil

"I want to go away to university 'cause you have to try and do something in a different area."
Male pupil

"You can have a better education and then when you get a job, yeah, they'll look at your file, to see if you're like good enough for it. Some of them, they'll just choose you 'cause you're good at things. You've got to have a good education to have a job."
Male pupil

"I want to get a paper round to get money."
Male pupil

Parents and grandparents viewed teenage years as a particularly perilous time, especially with respect to their children making decisions about substance abuse and friends.

"My main concern is just them getting in with the wrong crowds and growing up too soon. I just want them to be happy; I don't want them to do a disservice. I want them to do as well as they can at school."
Female parent

There was a degree of resignation about the inevitability of the challenges of teenage life:

"It's kind of inevitable. They become teenagers; you can't do much about it."
Female parent

"No sooner are you thinking, right they're safe to go out on their own, you're thinking are they gonna start drinking now?!"
Female parent

"I think it's important to be open about it and tell them what the consequences are of taking drugs or smoking or drinking or smoking or whatever. It's gonna be up to them to make their own decisions later on really, isn't it?"
Female parent

"I think it's the way you bring them up. Someone from a solid family background: I don't know 100 per cent but it has a lot of weight, the way you bring them up. My oldest grandson, I've got no problems with. He doesn't even like cigarettes. You know he comes from a smoking family and I smoke and his mum does. But I've got no feelings from him in regards of drugs or even alcohol."
Female grandparent

"Well, I'm a bit nervous about being a teenager 'cause there's loads of temptations, smoking and stuff."
Female pupil

"I was aware of drugs and all that sort of thing but certainly it seems to be more in your face though."
Female parent

At the same time there was a consensus among most of the parents and grandparents that today's children generally have more opportunities to pursue interests and make their own choices compared with their own youth:

"I mean what they have got now is fantastic. I take my grandson to the shows and he's got so many opportunities."
Female grandparent

"I think it's much more civilised now. I could only swim for the two months of the year around here when I was young. Now I've got a choice of swimming pools where I can go all times of the year. There are many more activities available to my grandchildren: they play tennis regularly and they skateboard – things like that. All the opportunities are there and, as a sports lover, I would have probably loved it."
Male grandparent

"It's more available for children these days mind, isn't it? More opportunities for them to go and get ahead."
Female parent

A few were conscious of persistent inequalities. As two Valleys grandparents put it:

"I help out in a different school about three mornings a week and they have 'circle time' on a Monday morning. The children start telling what they have done on the weekend and there's a fair half of those children in the one class who sit and watch the telly or play on their DS. They say: 'We didn't go nowhere, we didn't do nothing.' It's always the same little children, you know. Financially they haven't got a chance of going to places like our kids will go to. Other children have been to Cardiff shopping; parents will take them to different things and they do this and that."
Female grandparent

"When we were younger most of our parents' fathers were in the mine; all my friends' fathers were miners. The posh ones in my class were the fathers who worked in offices: white collar workers, you know. But to be honest they lived in ordinary terraced houses the same as us. I probably had as much as they did but you just felt because their father didn't work in the mines that they were better off."
Female grandparent

And one grandparent from Cardiff was concerned that the current academic system tends to favour the academically-minded:

"The education system has been developed to favour the academic students. That's not right because we need people to do lots of different kinds of jobs. Its not necessarily a good thing to have a degree unless its in something that's worthwhile. If you've got a degree and you can't get a job with it, what's the point in having a degree?"
Female grandparent

Chapter 5
Findings

1. Family life and relationships

The importance of talking was raised repeatedly during the focus groups. There was no doubt that the children valued those moments when they were listened to by people they trusted, especially their parents. Fewer children than the adults mentioned the need for 'quality time' but this need for attention was generally implicit or implied.

However, opportunities for unrushed time – 'quality time' – seemed fewer than many parents wished and fewer than they themselves said they had enjoyed as children. This is how one mother from the Valleys school put it:

"I'm always rushed and prioritising time. It's quality time with them that I lack. Sometimes I have to think what is quality time these days. Is it taking them somewhere? It's not really, is it? It's doing nothing with your children, just talking to them, and listening to them."

A mother from the Cardiff school said:

"I'm lucky. I only work for two days a week. It was a conscious decision to do that so I could spend time when the children were small. I've got friends that work full time and they are just constantly stressed about getting from work to make sure they spend enough time with the children. They feel guilty, so then they sign them up to all sorts of things, so I think I'm lucky in that sense."

Many of the adults admitted to being very pressed to find opportunities for 'quality time' with their children, which grandparents also observed represented a change over the generations. This is how one grandmother in Cardiff put it:

"I think sometimes the father in the situation - or sometimes it's the mother these days - has to work quite long hours and they come in late and they miss a lot of the children's childhood. My husband used to come in quite late, when the children were about 11 or 12. I very often had to go the parents' evenings on my own, because he was held up at work or he was working away, and that had an impact. He feels he missed out a lot on their childhood. I think that happens today too."

Mealtimes were widely regarded as important opportunities for families to get together and talk. However, many did not share meals, owing to practical difficulties or the unwillingness of family members to sit at a table. As one Valleys mother said:

"I've had a battle for the last 10 years since they were born. Dinner time has been terrible because they just won't sit at the table. I'm just hoping that eventually they will learn to sit at the table properly."

And a Cardiff grandmother observed:

"We used to have our meals on the table at teatime, and Sunday dinner and Sunday tea. We don't do that anymore. Most of the children I know don't do that anymore. It's trays on their lap in front of the TV."

Weekends provide a time when families can more easily capture the quality time that most parents we spoke with valued so much. As one Cardiff mother said:

"We always have a Sunday roast on Sunday. That's something I remember from my childhood and we've got back to it now. I would say meal times are very important and also bed times. My children are just avid book readers. It's a time for winding down as well, about an hour before bed. I would say they are quite important times."

There was variation in the involvement of grandparents according to place. In the Valleys focus group, for instance, many of the grandparents had lived in the area throughout the children's lives and were closely involved in bringing up their grandchildren. Quite a few grandparents and most parents had also attended the Primary School we visited in the Valleys. This contrasts quite markedly with the older generations in the north-east Wales and Cardiff focus groups. For example, only one parent at the Cardiff focus group was born in the city. A few grandparents in Cardiff and north-east Wales also said that they were involved in the day-to-day lives of their grandchildren but this was the case with all the grandparents in the Valleys focus group.

Two of the children's groups spoke about differences between boys and girls. At the Cardiff Primary approximately 50 per cent of the children are from ethnic minority backgrounds. The children in the focus group reflected on their identity in a candid and well informed fashion. The subject was raised spontaneously during a discussion about problems children discussed with parents, when one child mentioned racism. Probably due to the less ethnically diverse backgrounds of the children this subject was not raised in the north-east Wales or the Valleys focus groups.

2. Play and freedom

Two themes came up repeatedly during the group discussions about play, new technology and freedom to roam. Technological developments presented a significant change between the parents' and grandparents' generations and today's children.

The majority of children in every group mentioned that they enjoyed a mixture of television, games consoles and other electronic devices. However, it is possible to exaggerate the scale of these trends in children's lives: to believe, for example, that all children spend the majority of their time being passively amused by electronic gadgets. This was not the case with the children we interviewed. When asked their favourite place to play, and whether this was inside or outside the home, most of the children we spoke with opted for outdoor activities, playing as much outside as inside the home. As this Valleys boy said:

"It's better when you can go out to play than when you're stuck inside on a nice day."

And this north Wales boy added:

"Well, I like playing in the park mostly, playing football or netball, and I like taking the dog out and playing things like tag and hide and seek."

There was a strong and recurring sentiment among almost all parents and grandparents that children were not as free now to play without supervision or guidance, compared with their own experience. Both parents and grandparents spent a lot of time contrasting their memories of being allowed to play and roam freely in their neighbourhoods, to invent their own toys and activities, and to learn through unsupervised experiences, with the reality of today's constrictions.

Most of the adults we spoke with felt that the experience of childhood today had deteriorated as a result. In fact, when asked whether they would exchange their own childhood for what they observed as the experiences of today's children, all the adult groups declined, and all of them cited their relative freedom to roam as the main reason. Looking back one Valleys parent recalled:

"I think the best part of being a child was the freedom. You played in the street for hours or you went up the mountain for a picnic, whereas I find now I've got a nine year old little girl and unless she's got somebody's house to specifically be going to, or a club, you're very reluctant to say 'just go out and wander about'. I think most of her time would be spent going to different clubs or somebody else's house rather than just playing in the street. But streets are far busier now than they were when I was a child."

There was a good deal of discussion in the focus groups about why children have less freedom to roam these days, with different aspects being highlighted in different locations. In Cardiff, for instance, traffic was cited as a major concern, with this being less of a worry in the Valleys or north-east Wales. The children in the north seemed to be offered the most freedom, possibly because they lived in a semi-rural area. Children there said they regularly walked on their own to a friend's house.

However, in the Valleys and Cardiff children tended to be given lifts or escorted on foot to take part in activities or go to the homes of friends. Some children were allowed to play and roam, but with limitations. These included being accompanied by siblings or taking a mobile telephone to ensure they could be contacted. Traffic and parked cars featured highly in the minds of parents and grandparents.

In all the locations a significant number of respondents were conscious of 'stranger danger'. In north-east Wales one boy said:

"You're very safe in the house but outside even if you're comfortable with the place you still don't know if someone's going to jump out at you."

Without any prompting children in the Cardiff Primary used graphic terms to describe the potential dangers. Asked why she was not allowed out on her own one Cardiff girl responded:

"If you get kidnapped; or a man takes you, or a woman."

Another Cardiff girl said:

"I'm not allowed to go out really because my mum worries about me a lot. If we stay out a bit too long she worries and she goes really crazy and she goes outside trying to look for us, so that's why I normally have to go outside with my dad or with my mum."

Everywhere there was a feeling that 'stranger danger' had grown in perception in large part because of media coverage. For instance, some children in Cardiff referred spontaneously to the May 2007 Madeleine McCann case. This was when sustained media coverage was given to the disappearance of a four-year-old girl while on holiday in Portugal who had probably been abducted.

A mother at the Cardiff Primary school was among many who drew attention to the role of the media, which she said had completely changed the terms of the discussion:

"Today we have to bear the pain of the world, you know. Our parents, it was just the people they knew, but now it's everything: one disaster after another. Every child and parent has to take all that on-board and in a way that makes it very difficult to feel safe."

According to one north Wales father, media coverage was stifling children's development:

"There is a change. There's a change in society from the media. You have got to watch children more but I think as a society – I may be wrong - we've become overprotective. I do get annoyed. It goes back to risk; if you're never allowed to appreciate risk and become involved with risk how can you evaluate the risk? If you're constantly protected then you think you'll always be safe. And, of course, you're not because one day you'll be somewhere facing something and you won't be able to assess that risk. I do think we've gone too far, simply because of that."

The advent of cheaper mobile telephones represents a significant technological change between today's young generation and their parents and grandparents. The most obvious advantage for parents is that it allows them to keep tabs on their children remotely – and also serves as an emergency tool. In the Valleys especially, where a few children mentioned that they liked to roam the mountains and hills, children and their parents talked about mobile phones in this way. As one mother their put it:

"I think it's peace of mind for the child and the parents. Knowing that if they do get into trouble or they get lost or something, they can phone you. You can be looking at the clock, thinking you haven't spoken to him now for three hours maybe but you can just ring him to check he's okay. So it's peace of mind really isn't it?"

A Valleys boy said:

"If I take my mobile with me I tell my mother 'if you want me just phone me and I'll come back'."

However, in Cardiff, where parents and grandparents did not seem to often let their children roam, fewer children had mobiles. One parent commented:

"Mine would lose them; half a day and they'd lose them."

3. Boundaries and rules

The focus groups were asked to consider rules and boundaries in children's lives. Who makes them? How are they enforced? What sanctions are deployed when they are not observed? Parents and grandparents generally agreed that providing a structure or routine for children's lives was extremely important. At a basic level a routine ensured that children had sufficient sleep to prepare them for the following day.

Parents and grandparents across the focus groups thought negotiation on some matters was important to ensure that children were treated fairly. As one Valleys mother said:

"I think you got to be flexible, you got to treat them as individuals as well. I think they do feel a bit special when they have got the ability to make some decisions for themselves but you have to be sensible as well."

A Cardiff mother agreed:

"I know with my girls they don't always agree with the boundaries I put in place. I'm sure my daughter would love to sit at the computer on MSN until 2 o'clock. But we discuss these things and I think they understand the rules. On the other hand when I was growing it was just like do it and don't question it, which almost makes you push the boundaries."

Against the impression amongst most of the parents we spoke with that a good deal of negotiation went about rules and boundaries, the children generally thought they had less of an opportunity to participate. As these two boys, the first from the Valleys and the second from north Wales, put it:

"My mother says 'My roof, my rules'."

"There's no discussion about rules in our house."

One of the greatest generational shifts in discipline has been the disappearance of smacking. None of the parents and grandparents admitted to using smacking as a punishment. There seemed to be a consensus that it was an unacceptable form of discipline these days.

One change that a number of parents and grandparents referred to was the blurring of the boundaries between adults and children, particularly in the field of communication. The parents especially acknowledged that this development had occurred within their generation, and on the whole thought it a positive change.

Generally speaking, they thought their children had become more confident in expressing themselves and in addressing adults. Many recalled that they had been much more intimidated about expressing themselves confidently in this way, either for reasons of deference or fear. As one Cardiff grandmother put it:

"My daughter can say more things with me then I could say to my mum. There's a lot more openness when you talk to children. My grandchildren say things to me that I wouldn't dare say to my mother, certainly not my grandmother."

And a Cardiff mother added:

"Thirty years ago it wasn't considered that a child could have an opinion. Children were kind of a different species or they weren't quite human – a little subhuman. My parents would say: 'Oh, don't be silly, you can't have a headache'. Children behaved that way and it wasn't convenient for them. They were good parents and I had a happy childhood. But you were a child. You came in and you were told what to do by your mum or your dad unless you wanted to get into real trouble. I came from a family that still smacked."

A Valleys mother put the changes down to the schools:

"My children are a lot more confident than I was when I was their age. That's down to what they do in school. They're encouraged to speak in front of a group, whereas I would have died. It doesn't faze them at all. I think that's wonderful, especially when they're older."

And a Cardiff mother said:

"My children are more confident. I wasn't that confident at that age. I would definitely swap that. I would like to have been that confident."

There was variation in the application of rules and boundaries within families, with some children able to play off one parent against another. There was sometimes a mismatch between boundaries applied at home and school, the consequences of which had to be tackled primarily by teachers. For both parents and teachers there were also significant pressures from wider society that often seemed to run counter to their own intentions. Partly, this was age-old peer pressure, but also a feeling that there was a cultural pressure on children to grow up too quickly that was new. Many parents and grandparents felt children these days were being 'forced' – often by the media - to live like young adults in ways that were harmful.

The subject of boundaries and rules elicited strong responses from the older generation. Almost without exception grandparents in the study argued that behaviour and standards had deteriorated over time. However, it was not clear whether they were identifying a genuine social trend or simply recalling a perceived golden age when they were children. One point of agreement between both parents and grandparents was a perceived trend of declining standards of behaviour and courtesy in the public sphere generally, among adults as well as children.

A mixed picture emerged in the focus groups about boundaries and rules in children's lives day. There were common struggles that seem to have changed only a little over the generations. These included the importance of keeping a routine in children's lives, and trying to apply rules and boundaries consistently.

However, there was an overriding view that the increase in confidence amongst today's children compared with previous generations was positive since it led to their having a less inhibited and more comfortable relationship with their parents and grandparents. Today's children were able to discuss issues more openly and confidently. As a result today's parents thought they had a better relationship with their children than they had had with their parents.

4. The future

Every participant had views on the future. For the children, who were at the top end of primary school, the impending move to the unfamiliar surroundings of secondary school was generally viewed with some trepidation. Boys in particular were worried about bullying and encountering older children, as these comments, in turn from the Valleys, north Wales and Cardiff testify:

"I'm worried that I'm going to get bullied because my favourite lesson is science. I might get beat up and if I tell the teacher I might get beat up even more."

"I am frightened of being bullied."

"I'm scared they might make fun of me."

The Valleys children seemed particularly concerned. None voiced unequivocally positive thoughts about the transition to comprehensive school. One issue might be that they only had the choice of one, rather large secondary school. On the other hand the Cardiff children had a choice of several schools, while those in north-east Wales seemed more familiar with the Welsh-medium secondary school they would be attending.

Among the Valleys children there was a mixture of resignation and determination to make the best of a bad situation. At the same time all the children were looking forward to the prospect of the greater freedom they envisaged would result from reaching teenage years. As this Cardiff girl said:

"When you're a teenager you get more freedom. My parents tell me I'm not old enough yet to go out. We'll be able to go, like, clubbing and stuff."

At the Cardiff Primary parents spontaneously raised the issue of school choice, which was not mentioned at any other location by parents or grandparents. The children also compared schools and a few mentioned that friends had gone – or were intending to go - to different schools in the surrounding area. It was interesting that the

Cardiff parents did not appear to relish having to make choices about schools. As one female parent put it:

"Round here there are so many schools, people spread all over the place. It's this issue of choice. I don't want choice, I just want the local school to be good and for them to go there. I don't want to suddenly discover religion and have to send them somewhere else, which a lot of people do."

Most of the adults believed that their children and grandchildren have more opportunities in life and were generally more confident compared with themselves at a similar age. There was a consensus that today's children generally have more opportunities to pursue different interests and make their own choices.

At the same time, many were also pessimistic about the children's generally earlier involvement with society and the world. For many of the parents, and more so for grandparents, the world was fraught with dangers and temptations.

There was a widespread perception among both preceding generations that although many of the dangers children faced were not new, the extent and potential likelihood of the dangers, for example from drugs, were greater.

There was a degree of resignation about the inevitability of the challenges of teenage life. Many parents seemed to view the teenage years with the same dread and air of resignation, that some of the children displayed when talking about the move to secondary school.

At the same time parents and grandparents were generally optimistic about their children's development. They thought that children today had more opportunities to develop themselves and, with their greater confidence, should be able to take advantage of these opportunities in later life.

Chapter 6

Commentary

Let's get talking
Keith Towler, *Children's Commissioner for Wales*

This study by the Institute of Welsh Affairs gives us some compelling talking points:

- What role do the media play in portraying children and young people?

- Are parents and guardians giving children adequate freedom to play?

- What role should the state play in supporting lone parents to fulfil their work commitments and their role as parents?

- What are the burning issues facing children and young people in Wales?

In considering answers to these questions we need to think about potential solutions to some of the thorns in the side of society, including some adults' tendency to underestimate children's resilience. What's more, this report and the connected season of BBC programming provides an ideal opportunity to celebrate our children and young people and promote the positive impact they can have on society.

One of the great things about being the country's Children's Commissioner is that I get to talk about these things with people from across Wales and get to celebrate the achievements of children and young people all year round. However, my mind keeps returning to the same sticking point – whilst there are significant challenges we must face as a society, I can't help but wonder whether we adults are guilty of reflecting on our own childhood from behind rose-tinted glasses?

It is encouraging to read there was a consensus among most of the parents and grandparents questioned during this research that today's children generally have more opportunities to pursue interests and make their own choices compared to their own childhood.

This research brings to light that our children are more confident and many of the parents and grandparents thanked the style of schooling for this. It also brings to the fore the juggling act many parents and carers face between work commitments and family life. The majority of those questioned believed that spending 'quality time' with their children was essential.

My hope is that the BBC Wales season of programmes will give children and young people a voice. You could argue that they are the most important audience of all. In fact, children and young people have a right under the United Nations Convention on the Rights of the Child to have their voices and opinions heard when decisions are taken that could impact on their lives. Do we really know how they feel about growing up in Wales? Do we really know what their worries are? Are we adults really listening to what they have to say and taking steps to alleviate their concerns?

Childhood affects us all – we all have one – but what constitutes a good childhood? Let's get talking so we can share experiences and views and listen to each other. Talking is good and this focussed discussion provides a great opportunity to begin the development of a common understanding and appreciation of the wonder of childhood.

Diverse childhoods, participation and democracy: some reasons to be cheerful

Sally Holland, *School of Social Sciences, Cardiff University*

The participants in the focus groups, held in an inner city Cardiff primary school, a Valleys primary school, and a Welsh-medium school in a mixed urban and rural area in north-east Wales, raise issues that strike chords with many of the key debates in the social sciences today. In writing this reflection on the IWA report I briefly mention some of the recent debates in sociology about the position of children in society, and the state of the family. Secondly, I write about what I think some of these debates, and the important points raised by the children, parents and grand-parents in this study, might mean for social policy. In doing so, I pull out what I think are the many things to celebrate in this report, and suggest that perhaps we shouldn't be so gloomy about today's childhoods after all.

These focus groups provide an accessible and vivid snap-shot of the opinion of some children, parents and grandparents in contrasting locations in contemporary Wales. It is not a full research study, but the themes emerging from the groups' discussions are strikingly resonant with larger research studies and current debates in childhood studies.

Understanding trends in childhoods and families

Firstly, we need to be careful not to talk about 'children today' as if they are all the same and all have the same experiences. Childhoods are very diverse, not just between, say, India and Wales, but from community to community, and within communities too. In this report we can see how the local environment has the potential to strongly affect children's everyday experiences.

We can see that at least some children in the Valleys and rural areas still go up the mountain or call for friends to play. In the city, primary school children are perhaps more supervised due to traffic concerns. Some individual children in the Valleys will be escorted everywhere, whilst some in the city will be allowed to walk to school alone. The children in north Wales, who travel some distance to school, will have friends spread over a much wider geographical area than those attending school down the road. And of course it is not just parents' decisions that will affect children's experiences. Factors such as poverty, housing, disability, religion and culture all lead to varied experiences.

In the sociology of childhoods there is an emphasis on children's 'agency', that is children can act and make choices, they are not just passive recipients of adult behaviours. In this report we can see examples of children expressing their views quite clearly and parents commenting on how good it is that they are more confident to speak up and speak out than earlier generations were. We can also see examples of children's ability to act and think for themselves being constrained by adults' agendas, for example by having their out of school time more structured and supervised by adults.

Much has been written in the social sciences about our increasingly individualised society, with each of us pursuing our own life goals alongside more movement between jobs, between communities and even between partners. Some see these as contributing to a decline of the family. Others see societal changes as potentially bringing better ways of living, with more freedom to pursue different ways of 'doing' family life.

Much research in the UK suggests that many (but not all) families are becoming more democratic, with parents and children discussing things more and more equality between adult partners. This more democratic way of communicating with children is reflected in the focus groups in this study, with adults commenting that children have more of a say in families and in schools. But the parents and grandparents also express some ambivalence about how they organise their lives today, with some feeling pressurised to work long hours and see too little of their children as a result.

How can we build on the positives?

Some concerns were expressed by participants of all ages in this report. There were worries about children's safety outside the home, about parents' long working hours and about the transition to secondary school. On the other hand, there were many positives. Despite media panics about 'couch potato children', these children do play outside and want to do so more. We may be living in a more individualised society, but many of these children have the experience of extended family involved in their care, and parents do want to be spending more quality time with their children, not just pursuing material goals. Children are thought to be more confident and the older generations thought it was good that things are more informal now.

So, what changes do we need to make to society to build on these positives? One of the strongest themes coming out of the focus groups was that, although many children do still play outside, they do not have the freedom that their parents and grandparents did. Safe routes to school so that children can walk and cycle by themselves, 'home zones' where pedestrians take priority on residential streets, and a reduction in speed limits are the sort of measures that would ease some parental (and child) worries.

Social policies that make flexible working the norm for both fathers and mothers, and a change to how we talk and think about children's care so that it is seen as equally a concern for fathers as for mothers might help reduce some of the anxieties and burden that women feel. The debate should not be about whether women should work or not, but how whole families can be enabled to spend enough time together whilst still having an adequate income for their needs. The stark differences in maternity and paternity leave are a clear reminder that as a society we do not expect fathers to be too involved in children's care.

Lastly, in Wales we have made great strides in encouraging children's participation in society, from school councils to Funky Dragon. The adults in this focus group did not think that the children in their lives are disrespectful in speaking out more and being informal with adults. If we can continue to give children good experiences in playing a part in how decisions are made, then we are role-modelling respect, care and how to listen to others. We may learn something from them too.

Freedom to Play
Mike Greenaway, *Director, Play Wales*

What are we doing to our kids? This title might be perceived as accusatory, but perhaps rightly so. The Unicef Innocenti report into child poverty, produced in 2007, is an indictment of a UK society that appears to be developing a value system based on children being neither heard nor seen unless they are engaged in some activity that is deemed by adults to be meaningful and worthy.[4] However, for the children interviewed for this report perhaps the world is not quite so bad. This survey is, as it says, a snapshot in time of the views of nine small groups from across Wales, and while being a small sample there can be no doubt that much of what is said must surely ring true with most who read it.

Possibly the most significant finding, which perhaps should not come as a surprise, is that when asked to choose between their own childhood and childhood today, all the adult groups said that they would keep their own childhood because of the 'freedom to roam' they had as children. For many of us this must resonate with our own experience. Perhaps, if we reflected upon this as a society, we might begin to welcome the sight of children outside in our communities, just being and playing – rather than expecting that they must always be 'gainfully engaged'.

When we talk about childhood we find the conversation focuses so significantly on play. It may touch on many other areas that impact upon children but ultimately what is important to children is their play. Should this be a surprise? In successive consultations locally and nationally with children, it is always one of their top three issues.

As someone who has spent most of his working life with children there is no question of the authenticity of the views expressed. As a parent and grandparent much of what is said (particularly in respect of the increasing open relationships with successive generations) resonates with my own perceptions of family and the world.

I was intrigued with the finding that many children, while enjoying computer games, enjoyed playing actively outside just as much. This finding, in particular, deserves greater exploration in more extensive randomised research, to ascertain whether it is a feature specific to this sample of participants or whether it is more widespread. Perhaps, even with the narcotic like attraction of television and computers, we should anticipate that most children's favourite play spaces will be outside where there are a far wider range of features that allow for greater possibilities than those offered by the computer.

---

[4] UNICEF, Child poverty in perspective: An overview of child well-being in rich countries, Innocenti Report Card 7, 2007.

The perception of freedom across successive generations is in this report, defined by its loss. By implication this is a clear indication that freedom was valuable to everyone who participated and as such an essential part of childhood. In many instances this valued freedom is being replaced by adult organised and supervised activities for children. However, there appears to be a sense that children from the more rural areas still experience aspects of the freedom that defined the childhood of their parents and grandparents.

The other loss touched on, although not experienced everywhere, is perhaps best described as the loss of belonging, of being part of a wider community. We know this has a strong impact on children's confidence to play out. If children know the characters and characteristics of the community in which they live, if there is a sense of familiarity and acceptance, they are more likely to be happy to play out.

We might also have anticipated that traffic impacts upon children's opportunity to play outside. As a society we have failed our children. We have allowed public open space to become defined by our individual needs to move from one place to another as fast as possible. And on an immediate day-to-day level the price of our fast car dependency, is the loss of our children's freedom. This is surely fundamentally wrong. There needs to be a balance where children's rights and needs are accommodated and respected in the same way as those of adults.

The perception of the 'stranger danger' menace that lurks at every street corner is clearly a significant feature of the responses of many of those interviewed, regardless of their generation. With 24 hour news coverage, where good news is no news and stories of abducted children are used to boost newspaper sales, is it any wonder that we have developed an increasing perception that the world is a dangerous place? What we actually know, rather than feel, is that the world, with the notable exception of the dangers of increased numbers of cars and the speed of traffic, is no more a dangerous place than it was for the parents and grandparents.

While this report throws up some serious challenges for society and the way we provide for children and their play, it is nonetheless a positive report. However, I find myself wondering whether the positive perspective comes from the parents and grandparents rather than the children themselves. Returning to the Unicef report, it would be perverse to think that the freedom to play and the loss of it, did not contribute to children's perception of their wellbeing.

The Welsh Assembly Government was, in 2002, the first government to adopt a play policy in which it made a clear and aspirational commitment to children, to endeavour to meet their play needs. This report provides some evidence that there is a significant way to go.

A need to address gender differences and children's fears
Catriona Williams, *Chief Executive, Children in Wales*

There is an extremely marked gender bias in the comments from the focus groups in the IWA's report: 62 of the comments were attributed to mothers, whilst only six were attributed to fathers. This reflects the fact that fathers generally did not volunteer to take part in the focus groups. It is also broadly reflected in the comments from grandparents.

An alternative possibility exists, namely that the vast majority of those present came from single parent households. If this is the case, it begs the question as to how much input the separated fathers are having in the lives of their children, and how could they be better supported to increase this input. In either event it is probably fair to say that the report does not reflect an accurate picture of family life due to its gender bias among those who volunteered to take part.

Further work is needed to explore the reasons why fathers did not feel it appropriate to contribute to the discussions.

The role of grandparents in these families is also interesting. The comments support the findings of other research that all too often grandparents are acting in loco parentis, and are increasingly taking on the role of primary care giver. The old model of grandparents (of both genders) as people who offer quality time for their grandchildren is becoming increasingly rare.

This is undoubtedly a reflection of the much wider debate on work life balance in the 21st Century. This point was emphasised by the comments of the single parent mothers who find it ever more difficult to find quality time to spend with their children. Government policy which focuses on returning these women to work only exacerbates this problem. The report again supports other research in its finding that for many men work commitments are probably the biggest single barrier to their increased involvement with their children. The problem is further apparent in the comments that more and more of children's leisure time is now spent in organised activities.

Much more needs to be done in respect of affordable quality childcare, and more flexible working arrangements if these barriers are to be overcome.

The children's sense of gender identity is probably what would be expected from young people of this age group. However, their comments as to their fears and apprehensions, both in respect of the 'outside world', and also to the transition to secondary school is interesting. At present we make no differentiation in respect to gender, as to how we address fears of young people in these situations.

We have a duty to ensure that children and young people are not scared by the situations we put them in. We need to be looking at ways to address these fears not only in the wider context, but also in respect of the gender of that young person.

Appendix 1
Outline Profiles of the Schools Involved in the Study

Cardiff Primary School
This school, which serves part of the inner-city, has around 400 pupils. The areas around the school have pockets of economic deprivation, as indicated by the free school meal rate of close to 30 per cent (above the 19 per cent Welsh average). About half of the pupils come from ethnic minority backgrounds. As a result of the diversity of the school there are more than 10 languages spoken in pupils' homes.

Valleys Primary School
The school has just over 300 pupils, aged 3 - 11. About 20 per cent of the pupils receive free school meals. The area around the school is predominantly economically disadvantaged. English is the dominant language for almost all the pupils, and ethnic minority children are a tiny minority. Although none of the pupils speaks Welsh as a first language, there is a significant bilingual element and one assembly a week in the infant and junior departments is held in Welsh.

North-east Wales Primary school
There are around 250 pupils in the school, drawn from a mix of urban and rural areas. The school is designated Welsh-medium and so Welsh is the primary language for communication and lessons in the school. About 30 per cent of pupils come from a home where Welsh is the first language. The area is economically relatively well off, with only about 10 per cent of pupils receiving free school meals, well below the 19 per cent Welsh average.

Appendix 2
Project Steering Group

- **John Osmond,** *Director, IWA*
- **Nick Morris,** *Research Officer, IWA*
- **Huw Lewis,** *Secretary, IWA North Wales Branch*
- **Mandy Rose,** *Creative Director, Multiplatform, BBC Wales*
- **Belinda Herbert,** *Audience Research, BBC Wales*
- **Alun Shurmer,** *Head of Communications, BBC Wales*
- **Keith Towler,** *Children's Commissioner for Wales*
- **Sara Young,** *Media and PR Officer,*
  Office of the Children's Commissioner for Wales
- **Anne Crowley,** *Assistant Director for Policy and Research,*
  Save the Children Wales
- **Catriona Williams,** *Chief Executive, Children in Wales*
- **Professor Nigel Thomas,** *Professor of Childhood and Youth Research,*
  University of Central Lancashire
- **Dr Jonathan Scourfield,** *Childhood Research Group,*
  Cardiff University
- **Dr Sally Holland,** *Childhood Research Group,*
  Cardiff University
- **Melvyn Williams,** *Communications Manager,*
  Funky Dragon, the Children's and Young People's Assembly for Wales
- **Mike Greenaway,** *Director, Play Wales*